THE LIFE CYCLE OF A

Ladybug

By Colleen Sexton

BELLWETHER MEDIA • MINNEAPOLIS, MN

Note to Librarians, Teachers, and Parents:

Blastoff! Readers are carefully developed by literacy experts and combine standards-based content with developmentally appropriate text.

Level 1 provides the most support through repetition of high-frequency words, light text, predictable sentence patterns, and strong visual support.

Level 2 offers early readers a bit more challenge through varied simple sentences, increased text load, and less repetition of high-frequency words.

Level 3 advances early-fluent readers toward fluency through increased text and concept load, less reliance on visuals, longer sentences, and more literary language.

Level 4 builds reading stamina by providing more text per page, increased use of punctuation, greater variation in sentence patterns, and increasingly challenging vocabulary.

Level 5 encourages children to move from "learning to read" to "reading to learn" by providing even more text, varied writing styles, and less familiar topics.

Whichever book is right for your reader, Blastoff! Readers are the perfect books to build confidence and encourage a love of reading that will last a lifetime!

This edition first published in 2010 by Bellwether Media, Inc.

Library of Congress Cataloging-in-Publication Data
Sexton, Colleen A., 1967–
 The life cycle of a ladybug / by Colleen Sexton.
   p. cm. – (Blastoff! Readers life cycles)
 Includes bibliographical references and index.
 Summary: "Developed by literacy experts for students in kindergarten through grade three, this book follows ladybugs as they transform from eggs to adults. Through leveled text and related images, young readers will watch these creatures grow through every stage of life"–Provided by publisher.
 ISBN 978-1-60014-309-0 (hardcover : alk. paper)
 1. Ladybugs–Life cycles–Juvenile literature. I. Title.
 QL596.C65S49 2010
 595.76'9–dc22

                              2009037264

Printed in the United States of America, North Mankato, MN.
010110   1149

Contents

Ladybugs are **insects** that live in forests and fields.

There are more than 4,000 kinds of ladybugs. Each kind has its own colors and **patterns**. This ladybug is red with black spots.

Ladybugs grow in stages. The stages of a ladybug's **life cycle** are egg, **larva**, **pupa**, and adult.

egg

larva

pupa

adult

The egg breaks open and the larva twists out of the shell.

The larva rests. Its skin dries and hardens. The larva has a long body, six legs, and sharp jaws.

The larva uses its jaws to eat **aphids**. These tiny green insects move slowly. They are easy for the larva to catch.

The larva eats about 30 aphids a day!
It grows quickly. Soon the larva's skin is
too tight for its body.

The larva **molts**. Its skin splits open and the larva crawls out. The larva has a new skin that fits its bigger body.

The larva eats and grows. It molts again. The larva molts three times in all.

The larva stops eating when it is fully grown. It sticks the tail end of its body to a leaf and curls up.

The larva molts for the last time.
It changes into a pupa.

A case hardens around the pupa. The pupa changes into an adult inside the case.

The case breaks open and an adult ladybug crawls out. Its color is yellow at first.

The new adult rests for a day to let its wings dry. It changes color while it rests. The ladybug turns red and black.

The ladybug opens its wings.
It flies away to search for food
and to **mate**.

After mating the female lays her eggs. The tiny eggs are the start of a new life cycle!

Glossary

aphid—a tiny green insect that feeds on plants; ladybug larvae and adults eat aphids.

insect—a small animal with six legs and a body divided into three parts; there are more insects in the world than any other kind of animal.

larva—a young insect that hatches from an egg; the larva is the second stage of a ladybug's life.

life cycle—the stages of life of an animal; a life cycle includes being born, growing up, having young, and dying.

mate—to join together to produce young

molt—to shed skin so that a new skin can grow

pattern—shapes and colors that appear in a certain order; some ladybug patterns are red with black spots, black with red spots, and yellow with black spots.

pupa—the third stage of an insect's life when it turns from a larva into an adult; a ladybug pupa changes inside a hard case.

To Learn More

AT THE LIBRARY

Kalman, Bobbie. *Animal Life Cycles: Growing and Changing*. New York, N.Y.: Crabtree Publishing, 2006.

Miller, Heather Lynn. *This Is Your Life Cycle*. New York, N.Y.: Clarion Books, 2008.

Rustad, Martha E.H. *Ladybugs*. Minneapolis, Minn.: Bellwether Media, 2007.

ON THE WEB

Learning more about life cycles is as easy as 1, 2, 3.

1. Go to www.factsurfer.com.

2. Enter "life cycles" into the search box.

3. Click the "Surf" button and you will see a list of related Web sites.

With factsurfer.com, finding more information is just a click away.

Index